F*ck, I Died...Now What?

Practical Guide for Every Household

Michelle E Munger

In Memory Of

_____

"I'm not afraid of death; I just don't want to be there when it happens."
- Woody Allen

My Dearest

Hey, it's me, your friendly ghost scribbling you a letter from beyond the cosmic veil. Yep, I've crossed over to the other side, and let me tell you, the Wi-Fi here? Top-notch! Nothing but Netflix and chill 24/7. I wasn't really a fan of all those reality shows mind you, but then again, nothing is scripted here, and you get a little bit of everything. But enough about the afterlife perks; I've got a bone to pick with you!

Firstly, let's clear the air - I didn't exactly plan this whole "ghosting" thing, and if you are reading this, then something big and possibly bad happened to me, but there's no use crying over the past. I'd never want anyone to cry over me anyway...well, maybe just a few tears and then it's onwards and upwards. You don't have to worry about me anymore. I have an entire afterlife to get to know the world's greatest minds, travel the world, or just sit here with you.

I'm not going to throw any of that 'I'll love you till the end of time' shit at you because I know life is short and I want you to embrace it to the fullest. Find another special someone to spend the rest of your life with. God knows I would if it were me reading this. Didn't care much for the whole dying alone with all my cats scenario anyway.

I know you might still think that you can't do this without me, but you can. Trust me, I've see your superhero skills in action. You are a rockstar capable of handling anything life...or death...hurls at you. Just gather your wits, pull yourself up by your Doc Martin boot straps, and repeat after me: "I've got this. There isn't a thing in heaven or hell that can derail me." (I had to cover all the bases because we all know how hard heaven is to get into.)

So, wrap yourself in our memories like a cozy blanket, laugh until your sides hurt, and keep being the incredible human you are. I'll be the whisper in your ear when you are feeling lonely, the gentle breeze that smells like freshly cut grass and flowers to lift you up, or make you sneeze, whichever comes first. When life starts to get too serious, I'll be the soft tickle on your cheek, a reminder that YOU GOT THIS.

With infinite love, laughter, and a sprinkle of stardust,

- The Resident Ghost

Where to Start

Welcome aboard the emotional rollercoaster as we venture through the whirlwind of coping with the loss of a loved one. So, here's the deal: losing someone is like stepping into a dimension where the GPS doesn't work – you feel like you're navigating alone, and Google Maps is just as clueless as you are.

You've got to give yourself space to ugly-cry, scream into a pillow, or just eat a gallon of ice cream (no judgment here!). And don't forget to call up your personal squad of pals and family; they're the superheroes with the emergency emotional rescue kit.

Now, the practical stuff – alerting the authorities and sorting out the send-off shenanigans. Having a checklist handy is like having a Swiss Army knife in this emotional wilderness – seriously helpful!

Remember, there's no one-size-fits-all guidebook to grief. Take it at your own pace. Need a lifeline? Get yourself a pro, like a grief counselor or therapist – they're like emotional lifeguards in this sea of feelings. And believe it or not, the road to healing isn't a straight line; it's more like a twisted, tangled noodle.

Your loved one has no more problems anymore, they left that all behind for you to handle. Aren't you lucky. But here's the thing, even if you don't get everything 100% right, it'll still be fine.

You'll still have the memories of your loved one to sustain you whenever you start to feel sad. And speaking of memories, find quirky ways to honor them – like planting a disco-themed tree or organizing a karaoke night in their honor. There's no wrong way to memorialize your loved one...unless it's illegal. Don't do anything illegal.

Alright, let's face it - the Grim Reaper's schedule isn't exactly in our Google Calendar. So, when my time comes (hopefully not anytime soon), I want you to have the ultimate cheat sheet to avoid playing hide-and-seek with essential info. Think of this journal as your survival guide for when my eternal vacation finally happens.

Date of Death:

Hour of Death:

what the hell finally got me:

 Día de los Muertos

Imagine a world where the Day of the Dead, Día de los Muertos, is not just a day of remembrance but a living, breathing part of life. In this unique interpretation, the spirit of the celebration infuses every aspect of existence.

In this world, Día de los Muertos is not confined to a single day but is woven into the fabric of daily life. It's a world where the boundary between the living and the deceased is porous, and communication between the two realms is an everyday occurrence.

Families live in homes that are open, not just to the living but to the spirits of their ancestors. Altars adorned with marigold flowers and candles are maintained year-round to welcome these spirits. It's not uncommon to hear laughter and chatter as families share stories with their dearly departed over a cup of hot chocolate or a plate of tamales.

The cemeteries are not places of sorrow but bustling town squares. People picnic, dance, and sing as they celebrate with their deceased loved ones. The tombstones are vibrant works of art adorned with colorful mosaics, and the gravesites are tended as lovingly as gardens.

Artists are highly revered in this world, as they are the conduits of communication between the realms. They paint murals of the deceased, capturing their essence in vivid detail. These murals are not static but are believed to come to life during Día de los Muertos, allowing the spirits to briefly inhabit them.

Food vendors line the streets, offering not only earthly delights but also dishes beloved by the deceased. It's a world where taste and smell can transport you back to cherished memories with those who have passed.

In this unique take on Día de los Muertos, death is not feared but embraced. It's a celebration of life and an ongoing conversation with those who have come before, reminding us that they are never truly gone as long as they live in our hearts and in the vibrant tapestry of existence.

Writing an Obituary

Begin this heartfelt homage by meticulously assembling the vital details that frame the remarkable narrative of your dearly departed - their full name, the day they bravely embarked on life's grand adventure, the day the cosmic GPS rerouted their path, and the geographical coordinates where they penned their final chapter.

Next, craft the intricate family tree that branched through their existence: the devoted partner who shared their heart's secrets, the rambunctious offspring who inherited their quirks, the adorable grandchildren who melted their stern façade, and the constellation of relatives who added hues to their life's mural. These are the characters in the play that was their existence.

Choose a Tone and Style:

Now, contemplate the overall tone of this tribute. Obituaries are like the final notes in life's symphony, each with its unique melody. They can be as dignified as a Shakespearean soliloquy or as intimate as a late-night chat with a close friend, depending on your preference and the departed's personality.

As for the length of this farewell sonnet, some are concise as haikus, capturing the essence in a few brushstrokes, while others stretch into epic sagas, painting a vivid mural of the departed's odyssey. The chosen length, much like the curtain call of a theater performance, reflects the reverence for the life that was lived and the legacy that endures.

Write the Obituary:

Embark on this heartfelt tribute by respectfully pronouncing the full name of your beloved traveler, their age at the time they embarked on their cosmic journey, the poignant location where their earthly pilgrimage reached its final destination, and the date when the universe bade them adieu.

If you're feeling up to it, dive into the epic tale of where it all began - their hometown and the brave souls who spawned them, also known as their parents (the folks who gave them life and a lifelong aversion to broccoli).

Now, let's chronicle the highlights of this grand adventure we call existence - from those thrilling school days when they mastered the art of trading sandwiches, to the soaring heights of their career (or at least that one time they were Employee of the Month). Don't forget to throw in some lovey-dovey bits about that magical day when they said, "I do," and made a lifelong commitment to sharing the TV remote.

Let's not neglect their inner world either - their hobbies, passions, and obsessions that made them the quirky, lovable soul they were. Did they collect stamps shaped like famous vegetables? Or perhaps they had a secret talent for juggling flaming marshmallows.

But wait, there's more! It's time to give a shout-out to the supporting cast - the adoring spouse, the adorable offspring, the pint-sized grandkids who knew how to work those puppy-dog eyes. And of course, let's not forget to acknowledge the ancestors who set the stage for this remarkable performance.

Now, on to the grand finale - the ultimate farewell party. Make sure to spill the beans about when and where this extravaganza of memories will take place. If the departed had a preference for roses over lilies or donations to the "Save the Endangered Gummy Bear Foundation," this is the place to spill the secrets.

As the curtain falls on this heartfelt tribute, throw in a few words of thanks for the indelible mark they left on the world and a plea for warm thoughts, kind words, and maybe even a casserole or two from the neighbors. Let's proofread this masterpiece with the meticulousness of an eagle-eyed grammar guru to ensure that every "i" is dotted, every "t" is crossed, and every punchline lands with perfect comedic timing.

Absolutely, let's put the "snap" in snapshot for this next bit. If you can rustle up a recent photo of the dear departed, it's like the icing on the obituary cake. Not only does it remind folks of their lovely visage, but it's a visual testament to the fact that they really did exist in a world of pixels and hashtags.

Now, as for the grand unveiling of this obituary masterpiece, you've got options galore. You can go old-school and grace the hallowed pages of newspapers. Or, you can venture into the wild, wild west of the internet, where online memorial sites await your digital brush strokes. And hey, why not let social media join the party? After all, there's nothing like broadcasting your heartfelt tribute to the masses in 280 characters or less.

Before you send this digital masterpiece off into the cyberspace, let's read the fine print. Each platform has its own quirks and rules. It's like showing up to a costume party and realizing it's a black-tie event - you've got to know the dress code. So, do your due diligence, my friend, and make sure you're ticking all the right boxes.

Now, here comes the fun part - spreading the news! Email it to Aunt Mildred, post it on your cousin's Facebook wall, and send it via carrier pigeon if that's your style. The goal here is to ensure that everyone who ever had a chat, a chuckle, or a cup of tea with the departed gets to share in this beautiful farewell. Let's do this with the grace of a synchronized swimmer and the precision of a chess grandmaster.

Sample Obituaries

The galaxy is a bit dimmer today as we bid farewell to Darth Vader, a man who wore his love for dramatic entrances and deep breathing on his mechanical sleeve. Born as Anakin Skywalker, he later donned the iconic black suit and cape, and a villainous legacy was born (literally, with the help of a volcano).

Darth Vader was many things: a Jedi Knight, a podracing enthusiast, and an expert at force-choking subordinates who couldn't properly file TPS reports on the Death Star. He had an uncanny ability to turn any conversation into a discussion about the power of the Dark Side and could effortlessly win any father-son argument with the revelation, "I am your father."

Despite his menacing exterior, Darth Vader had a softer side. He was a family man, in his own way, and was known to enjoy bonding moments with his children, even if those moments usually involved trying to convert them to the Dark Side.

He had an unusual passion for interior decorating, and his choice of black for everything, from his Star Destroyer to his coffee mugs, showed a consistent commitment to his aesthetic.

In his later years, he found a new lease on life as a force ghost, and we'd like to think he's finally found some peace (or at least learned how to have a good laugh).

Darth Vader may have been the ultimate Sith Lord, but in the end, his journey reminds us that even the darkest of hearts can find redemption. So, as we remember him today, let's celebrate the man who brought balance to the Force in his own unique way. May the Force be with you, Darth Vader, as you embark on your next adventure in a galaxy far, far away. 🌠🪐 👓 #RIPDarthVader

What's up, doc? Well, apparently, not much anymore. We gather here today to bid farewell to the one and only Bugs Bunny, the carrot-chomping, wisecracking rabbit who kept us laughing for generations.

Born in a carrot patch somewhere in the depths of Looney Tunes Land, Bugs quickly rose to stardom with his trademark catchphrases and iconic carrot consumption. He was the ultimate prankster, always one step ahead of Elmer Fudd and Yosemite Sam. And let's not forget his cross-dressing escapades; he rocked a dress better than anyone in history!

Bugs had an unquenchable thirst for carrots that rivaled a vampire's thirst for blood. He once traded a solid gold carrot for a lifetime supply of his favorite orange snack, proving that you can't put a price on a rabbit's true love.

Despite his mischievous nature, Bugs had a heart of gold. He was known to help out his fellow toons in times of trouble, whether it was Daffy Duck's latest debacle or Porky Pig's perpetual stutter.

In his downtime, Bugs enjoyed carrot smoothies, long walks through Acme Acres, and performing stand-up comedy at the local "Hare-raising" comedy club. He was a connoisseur of classical music, with a particular fondness for Wagner (even though he thought it was "wabbit season").

So here's to you, Bugs Bunny, the wabbit who taught us that it's okay to be a little wacky in this crazy world. May your carrot patch in the sky be forever bountiful, and may you keep the angels in stitches with your hare-larious jokes. What a maroon we'll be without you! 🥕 🐰 ✴ #RIPBugsBunny

Take a few moments to write your own or your loved ones obituary. Place pictures that you like of the deceased within these pages, or if you are writing your own obituary, place the pictures you think represent you the most.

Hinduism Belief on Death

In Hinduism, the journey through life and death is an intricate dance of karma, dharma, and reincarnation. Imagine life as a grand theater production, with each soul taking its turn on the cosmic stage.

When a soul's performance in one life comes to an end, it's time for an encore in another. This process of reincarnation is like a never-ending cycle of auditions, with the ultimate goal being liberation from the stage itself.

Karma, the law of cause and effect, is the director of this cosmic play. Every action, good or bad, has its consequences – setting the stage for future acts. It's like a universal theater critic, always keeping tabs on the actors.

Dharma, on the other hand, is the script of life. It's the role each soul must play in the grand production. Whether you're a hero or a sidekick, embracing your role with grace and fulfilling your duty is the key to a stellar performance.

Now, let's talk about Moksha – the grand finale! When a soul has perfected its act, it's time to exit the stage and join the cosmic audience. It's like winning an Oscar and retiring to enjoy the show.

So, in Hinduism, life, death, and reincarnation are part of an epic drama where each of us is both the actor and the audience, striving for the perfect performance that earns us a standing ovation in the universe's grand theater.

Important People

In this quirky scrapbook, you'll find a motley crew of characters I've encountered in my wacky life adventure. It's like my personal Hall of Fame, but with more chaos and fewer trophies. To all you folks whose names grace these pages, consider yourselves my honorary co-stars in the movie of my life. You've each earned a backstage pass to the theater of my heart, where you'll forever have VIP status!

Name

Address

Telephone Number

E-mail Address

Name

Address

Telephone Number

E-mail Address

Name

Address

Telephone Number

E-mail Address

Name

Address

Telephone Number

E-mail Address

Important People

Name

Address

Telephone Number

E-mail Address

Name

Address

Telephone Number

E-mail Address

Name

Address

Telephone Number

E-mail Address

Name

Address

Telephone Number

E-mail Address

Name

Address

Telephone Number

E-mail Address

Important People

Name
_____

Address
_____

Telephone Number
_____

E-mail Address
_____

Name
_____

Address
_____

Telephone Number
_____

E-mail Address
_____

Name
_____

Address
_____

Telephone Number
_____

E-mail Address
_____

Name
_____

Address
_____

Telephone Number
_____

E-mail Address
_____

Name
_____

Address
_____

Telephone Number
_____

E-mail Address
_____

Important People

Name
_____

Address
_____

Telephone Number
_____

E-mail Address
_____

Name
_____

Address
_____

Telephone Number
_____

E-mail Address
_____

Name
_____

Address
_____

Telephone Number
_____

E-mail Address
_____

Name
_____

Address
_____

Telephone Number
_____

E-mail Address
_____

Name
_____

Address
_____

Telephone Number
_____

E-mail Address
_____

Important People

Name
_____

Address
_____

Telephone Number
_____

E-mail Address
_____

Name
_____

Address
_____

Telephone Number
_____

E-mail Address
_____

Name
_____

Address
_____

Telephone Number
_____

E-mail Address
_____

Name
_____

Address
_____

Telephone Number
_____

E-mail Address
_____

Name
_____

Address
_____

Telephone Number
_____

E-mail Address
_____

Important People

Name

Address

Telephone Number

E-mail Address

Name

Address

Telephone Number

E-mail Address

Name

Address

Telephone Number

E-mail Address

Name

Address

Telephone Number

E-mail Address

Name

Address

Telephone Number

E-mail Address

Important People

Name

Address

Telephone Number

E-mail Address

Name

Address

Telephone Number

E-mail Address

Name

Address

Telephone Number

E-mail Address

Name

Address

Telephone Number

E-mail Address

Name

Address

Telephone Number

E-mail Address

Important People

Name
_____

Address
_____

Telephone Number
_____

E-mail Address
_____

Name
_____

Address
_____

Telephone Number
_____

E-mail Address
_____

Name
_____

Address
_____

Telephone Number
_____

E-mail Address
_____

Name
_____

Address
_____

Telephone Number
_____

E-mail Address
_____

Name
_____

Address
_____

Telephone Number
_____

E-mail Address
_____

Important People

Name

Address

Telephone Number

E-mail Address

Name

Address

Telephone Number

E-mail Address

Name

Address

Telephone Number

E-mail Address

Name

Address

Telephone Number

E-mail Address

Name

Address

Telephone Number

E-mail Address

Important People

Name

Address

Telephone Number

E-mail Address

Name

Address

Telephone Number

E-mail Address

Name

Address

Telephone Number

E-mail Address

Name

Address

Telephone Number

E-mail Address

Name

Address

Telephone Number

E-mail Address

Important People

Name

Address

Telephone Number

E-mail Address

Name

Address

Telephone Number

E-mail Address

Name

Address

Telephone Number

E-mail Address

Name

Address

Telephone Number

E-mail Address

Name

Address

Telephone Number

E-mail Address

Important People

Name
_____

Address
_____

Telephone Number
_____

E-mail Address
_____

Name
_____

Address
_____

Telephone Number
_____

E-mail Address
_____

Name
_____

Address
_____

Telephone Number
_____

E-mail Address
_____

Name
_____

Address
_____

Telephone Number
_____

E-mail Address
_____

Name
_____

Address
_____

Telephone Number
_____

E-mail Address
_____

Important People

Name

Address

Telephone Number

E-mail Address

Name

Address

Telephone Number

E-mail Address

Name

Address

Telephone Number

E-mail Address

Name

Address

Telephone Number

E-mail Address

Name

Address

Telephone Number

E-mail Address

Japanese Buddhism

In the heart of Japanese Buddhism lies a profound dance with death, where life and the afterlife perform a delicate waltz.

Picture a serene Japanese garden, with its meticulous balance of elements – the lush, living greenery and the contemplative stillness of stone gardens. This duality mirrors the Japanese approach to death.

Buddhism, the guiding philosophy, weaves the belief in reincarnation and the concept of impermanence into the cultural fabric. Life is fleeting, like cherry blossoms carried away by a gentle breeze.

Japanese funerals are as much about celebrating life as they are about acknowledging death. It's a solemn affair, where family and friends gather to honor the departed. But, it's also filled with rituals like the burning of incense, the offering of food, and the lighting of lanterns, illuminating the path to the next world.

In this unique cultural tapestry, ancestors are revered and remembered through ancestral altars. They remain an integral part of family life, a source of guidance, and a connection to the spiritual realm.

Cemeteries, often nestled in tranquil natural settings, are places of reflection and meditation. They are where the living can commune with the departed and pay their respects.

Japanese death culture encapsulates a profound acceptance of mortality, an embrace of the transient nature of existence, and a belief in the eternal continuation of the soul's journey – all within the tranquility and beauty of a Zen garden.

How I Want to be Buried

How I Want to be Buried

In-Ground Burial (Traditional Burial):

Ah, the classic burial style - it's like the evergreen of farewells! Picture your loved one cozied up in a casket, in a fancy spot at the cemetery. You've got choices, like singles for lone wolves or doubles for the "till death do us part" folks. Now, about those double plots – hey, love happens, and you don't want any ghostly marital drama, so let's chat about what if they decide to say "I do" beyond the grave.

Above-Ground Burial:

Some cemeteries are offering the high-rise option for our dear departed. It's like the luxury condo of afterlife real estate. We're talking mausoleums and columbariums, where you can stash caskets or urns like it's an above-ground treasure hunt. The best part? No muddy feet for your loved one – it's like the VIP treatment. This is the go-to choice for those places where the ground has a bit of an attitude problem. You know, when it just won't cooperate with traditional burials. So, up, up, and away we go!

Green Burial (Natural Burial):

Say hello to the eco-warrior of burials! Green burials are all about keeping Mother Earth happy. No embalming fluids or plastic materials here - we're going au naturel. Picture this: your loved one becomes one with nature in a green cemetery or a serene natural preserve. It's like joining an exclusive club for environmentally-conscious afterlife enthusiasts. Plus, you get to give back to the planet as a thank-you note for all the years you spent on it. Go green or go home!

Cremation:

Let's talk about the sizzling trend in afterlife fashion – cremation! We're talking about turning your loved ones into ashes. But here's the twist: you can get creative with it! These ashes can hang out in an urn, go on a scenic tour, chill in a cemetery, or even become the bling of the afterlife with some fancy memorial jewelry. Some companies are taking it up a notch. Ever heard of ashes in concrete? They're literally building coral reefs with your Aunt Mildred! And don't get me started on the everlasting diamonds – the inheritance of the future! So, whether your loved one wants to travel, shine, or become a piece of underwater real estate, cremation has it all.

Home Burial:

Ever fancied having your very own cemetery right in your backyard? In some places, you can host your own burial bash on your private property. But hold your horses; it's not a free-for-all. You might need to cozy up to some local laws and use those fancy biodegradable caskets, because we're all about being eco-friendly even in the great beyond. So, if you've got a green thumb and a spacious backyard, why not turn it into a final resting place?

Cemetery Options:

A cemetery is basically a melting pot of various religious and cultural groups. It's like a buffet, but for the afterlife! You've got sections for every belief system under the sun, from A to Z, and everything in between. And guess what? Some of these places even come with bonus features like bench memorials and tree planting options. It's like adding extra toppings to your sundae! So, whether you're sharing a spot with a neighbor or planting your roots on your ancestral turf, the options are as diverse as your dearly departed pals!

Veterans' Cemeteries:

Picture this: a place where veterans and their kin get the VIP treatment even after they've hung up their boots. It's like a special club, but without the secret handshake. Uncle Sam's Department of Veterans Affairs runs  the show here, and they don't skimp on the perks. It's like an exclusive party for those who've served their country, and the best part? Family members can join in on the fun too! So, when the time comes, veterans and their loved ones can rest easy knowing they've got a place in one of these elite resting spots. It's like the ultimate salute to a life well-lived.

Sea Burial (Burial at Sea):

Ahoy there, sea lovers! If you've ever dreamed of giving the fishies a snack, consider this: a sea burial, the ultimate oceanic adventure! Imagine your ashes drifting off into the deep blue, as you become one with the great abyss. Just remember, the sea is a stickler for rules, so you'll need permits aplenty to pull off this aquatic escapade. But once you've navigated the bureaucratic waters, you're free to let your loved one rest in the bosom of Poseidon's kingdom. It's a watery send-off that's eco-friendly and as vast as the horizon itself. So, for those who truly have saltwater in their veins, this is the way to make a splashy exit!

Donate to Science

Explore the option of donating your body to science, where medical colleges seek cadavers for research purposes. Alternatively, you can opt to contribute to a body farm—a facility dedicated to studying natural decomposition processes.

By choosing this path, your remains could aid in crucial forensic research, providing valuable insights into crime-solving methodologies even beyond your life. This noble choice not only advances scientific understanding but also contributes significantly to society's quest for knowledge and justice.

Here's the scoop: what happens to these old bones is a bit of a "choose your own adventure." You can toast me up like a marshmallow, plant me like a tree, or offer me up as a guinea pig for science – it's all fair game! But here's the kicker: I've got my own preference. Drumroll, please...

Tibetan Buddhism

In the high, windswept plateaus of Tibet, where the sky touches the earth and prayers seem to linger in the thin mountain air, Tibetan Buddhism and its death rituals take on a unique and profound character.

Tibetan Buddhists believe in the cycle of reincarnation, where death is merely a bridge from one life to the next. The journey through this cycle is guided by the Bardo Thodol, known as the Tibetan Book of the Dead. It is said to be read to the deceased to help them navigate the afterlife's complexities.

Death in Tibet is seen as a transformation, a continuation of the soul's path. The deceased's body is treated with great care, often brought to a mountaintop to be exposed to the elements and vultures in what's known as a "sky burial." This practice, which may seem macabre to some, aligns with the Buddhist belief in impermanence and the interconnectedness of life and death.

But the rituals don't end there. In the charming and ornate monasteries that dot the Tibetan landscape, butter lamps are lit to guide the soul, and intricate mandalas are created and then ritually destroyed to signify the fleeting nature of life's beauty.

Tibetan Buddhists have a poignant and pragmatic way of looking at death. It's neither feared nor denied; instead, it's embraced as a natural part of existence, like the ever-turning prayer wheels that scatter blessings with each spin.

In the land where the earth meets the heavens, death is but a passage to another part of the cosmic dance, and Tibetan Buddhism ensures the steps are taken with reverence, wisdom, and deep spiritual insight.

Life
Insurance

Importance of Life Insurance

Life insurance, it's like the superhero cape of financial planning!

Picture this: You're the head of the household, the chief breadwinner, the one who knows the secret recipe for the world's best mac 'n' cheese. Now, what if, heaven forbid, you're suddenly not around to whip up that cheesy masterpiece anymore? That's where life insurance swoops in to save the day!

Life insurance isn't just a fancy piece of paper; it's your safety net, your financial guardian angel. You see, it's all about making sure your loved ones don't find themselves in hot water if you're not there to pay the bills. Mortgage? Covered. Kid's college fund? Covered. Those pesky credit card debts? You guessed it, covered!

But life insurance isn't just about paying the bills; it's like a GPS for your family's future. It ensures your spouse can still sip piña coladas on a beach somewhere when they retire, and your kids can become rocket scientists or professional ice cream tasters.

So, in a nutshell, life insurance is your way of saying, "Hey, family, I've got your back, even from the great beyond!" It's the financial superhero that keeps your loved ones flying high, long after you've hung up your cape.

Life Insurance

Gather Important Documents:

Gather all pertinent documentation that might hold information related to the life insurance policy you're seeking. Consider scouring through various documents encompassing financial records, bank statements, tax returns, and any correspondence exchanged with insurance companies.

Financial records might disclose premium payments made to the insurer, while bank statements could potentially reveal transactions linked to insurance premiums or policy-related deductions. Tax returns often contain details about deductible premiums or income tax benefits related to life insurance policies. Furthermore, letters, emails, or notices from insurance providers might offer valuable insights into policy details, premium payments, or policyholder information.

By meticulously examining these documents, you enhance the likelihood of unearthing relevant information about the life insurance policy, enabling a comprehensive understanding of its terms, coverage, beneficiaries, and payout details.

Check Safe Deposit Boxes and Personal Records:

Scour through your loved one's personal records, meticulously examining paper files, address books, and notepads for any potential clues pertaining to a life insurance policy. Additionally, explore the possibility of them having a safe deposit box at a bank, as these secure compartments often serve as storage for important documents, including life insurance policies.

Within personal files, look for any paperwork, contracts, or statements that might indicate a life insurance policy's existence. Address books or contact lists might contain information about insurance agents or companies, providing leads to uncover pertinent policies. Furthermore, handwritten notes or annotations within documents could hint at insurance-related matters.

Contact the Insurance Agent:

If you possess information about the insurance company and the specific agent your loved one collaborated with, initiating contact with the agent can be a beneficial step in obtaining assistance. Furnish the agent with as much pertinent information as possible, such as the policyholder's complete name, date of birth, and Social Security number, if available.

Engage with the insurance agent by elaborating on the details you've gathered, including any policy-related documentation or clues, to help streamline the search process. Providing additional context, such as the policy's issue date, any associated beneficiaries, or premium payment history, could expedite the agent's efforts in locating the life insurance policy.

Review Mail and Emails:

Look through your loved one's recent mail and emails for any correspondence from insurance companies. This may include premium notices or statements.

Search Online Policy Locator Services:

Several insurance companies provide online tools or dedicated policy locator services designed specifically to assist beneficiaries in locating policies. Verify whether the insurer offers such a beneficial service to aid in your search for the life insurance policy.

Explore the insurer's website or contact their customer service department to inquire about available policy locator tools or online resources. These platforms might offer search functionalities or dedicated portals where beneficiaries can input relevant information, such as the policyholder's details, in an attempt to track down existing policies.

Check State Insurance Departments:

Each state has an insurance department that may help you locate a policy if you have the insurer's name. You can find contact information for your state's insurance department online.

Review Bank Statements and Cancelled Checks:

Look for any payments made to an insurance company on your loved one's bank statements or cancelled checks. You should also call the bank and have them do a seaarch for you on the bank account if you can't find the records..

Contact Previous Employers:

If your loved one held employer-sponsored life insurance, reaching out to their previous employers' Human Resources (HR) departments can be an essential step in your quest to uncover potential policies.

Initiate contact with the HR departments of your loved one's past employers to inquire about any existing life insurance policies provided as part of their employment benefits. Provide comprehensive details, including the individual's full name, employment dates, and any relevant identification numbers or documents, to aid the HR personnel in locating potential policies

Engaging with these HR departments can yield crucial information regarding employer-sponsored life insurance policies held by the deceased. By leveraging this avenue, you may access valuable insights into any policies in place, ensuring a thorough exploration of all potential avenues to identify and claim existing life insurance benefits.

Examine Credit Reports:

Obtain your loved one's credit reports to glean insights into potential financial commitments or continued payments made to insurance companies. These credit reports often offer visibility into outstanding debts and recurring payments, shedding light on any active relationships with insurance providers.

Consult the MIB (Medical Information Bureau):

The MIB functions as a database utilized by insurance companies to exchange medical condition details.
Additionally, it might harbor data about life insurance policies associated with the individual. Submitting a request to the MIB, albeit for a fee, can potentially yield valuable information pertinent to uncovering any existing life insurance policies held by the deceased.

Ask Family and Friends:

Speak with close friends and other family members who might possess insights into the policy or have been beneficiaries themselves. Their shared experiences or knowledge could offer valuable information regarding any existing life insurance policies held by the deceased.

Hire a Professional Locator:

If your search for the policy proves unsuccessful, contemplate enlisting the services of a specialized professional locator or investigator adept at tracing unclaimed insurance policies. Their expertise in this field might provide additional avenues for uncovering the elusive life insurance policy.

Check Unclaimed Property Databases:

Certain states maintain unclaimed property databases that could potentially feature unclaimed life insurance policies. You can access these databases online and conduct searches to determine if any unclaimed life insurance policies belonging to your loved one have been listed.

Be Patient and Persistent:

Locating a lost life insurance policy can take time, especially if your loved one kept their financial affairs private. Be patient and persistent in your search.

Once you've located the policy, contact the insurance company's claims department and follow their instructions for filing a claim. Provide all necessary documentation, including a death certificate and proof of your status as a beneficiary. Keep copies of all communications and documents related to the claim process.

Life Insurance Company

Contact Information

Ghanaian Fantasy Coffins

In the vibrant and colorful world of Ghanaian Fantasy Coffins, death becomes a celebration of life like no other.

Imagine a world where coffins are not mere vessels for the deceased but exquisite works of art that reflect a person's life, passions, and achievements. In Ghana, this is not a dream but a reality, and these fantastical coffins, also known as "abebuu adekai," are at the heart of their unique funeral culture.

Each fantasy coffin is a masterpiece, meticulously crafted to honor the deceased in a truly personalized way. Whether it's a giant fish for a fisherman, a camera for a photographer, or a Mercedes-Benz for a car enthusiast, these coffins encapsulate the essence of the departed's life. It's as if their spirit lives on in these remarkable creations.

Ghanaian funerals are vibrant affairs filled with music, dancing, and storytelling. People come together not to mourn but to celebrate the life that once was. The fantasy coffins take center stage in this grand spectacle, paraded through the streets, accompanied by joyous songs and jubilant dances. It's a send-off that truly befits the unique character of the deceased.

The Ghanaian belief is that death is not an end but a transition, and these whimsical coffins are a testament to that. They remind us that life, in all its colors and eccentricities, should be celebrated and cherished, even in the face of death. In Ghana, funerals are not about saying goodbye but about sending the departed off with style, flair, and a whole lot of heart.

Last
Will

Last Will

Your last will and testament is like the ultimate roadmap for your grand exit. It's not just any map; it's the GPS of life's final journey, complete with all the critical pit stops.

You see, this document is your chance to drop some knowledge bombs, telling your family and friends exactly how you want things to go down after you've left the building. From who gets your prized collection of vintage action figures (because, let's face it, they're priceless) to who's in charge of the family fortune (cha-ching!), your will is your chance to drop the mic and leave no room for confusion.

Now, let's talk about the kids. Your will is like the magical spellbook that appoints guardians for your little wizards-in-training. Without it, you're leaving the decision to chance, like playing a game of musical chairs where nobody wins.

So, in a nutshell, your last will is your ultimate script for the grand finale. It's the peacekeeper, the treasure map, and the storyteller all rolled into one. It ensures your wishes are crystal clear, your assets go where they should, and your loved ones aren't left in a real-life soap opera plot twist. It's like your final mic drop, but in legal document form.

Making a Last Will

Gather Information:

* Make a list of your assets, including real estate, bank accounts, investments, personal property, and valuable items.
* Identify your beneficiaries, including family members, friends, and any charitable organizations you wish to include.
* Decide on an executor, the person responsible for carrying out your wishes as stated in the will.

Choose an Executor:

* Select a responsible and trustworthy person to act as your executor. This individual will manage your estate, pay debts, and distribute assets according to your will.
* Discuss your decision with the chosen executor and ensure they are willing to take on this role.

Draft the Will:

* Begin by stating that you are of sound mind and writing your will voluntarily. This is to establish that you are creating the document willingly and without coercion.
* Clearly state that this document is your "Last Will and Testament" and that it revokes any previous wills you may have written.
* Specify your name, address, and any other relevant identification details.

Assign Guardianship (if applicable):

* If you have minor children or dependents, designate a legal guardian(s) in your will to ensure their care and well-being in the event of your passing.

Detail the Distribution of Assets:

* Outline how you want your assets to be distributed among your beneficiaries. Be specific in naming beneficiaries and their respective shares or assets.
* Consider contingencies, such as what should happen if a beneficiary predeceases you.

Include Specific Bequests:

* Specify any valuable or sentimental items you want to leave to specific individuals.
* Clearly state who should receive each item and describe the item with sufficient detail for easy identification.

Address Debts and Taxes:

* Indicate how you want your debts, including outstanding loans, mortgages, and credit card balances, to be paid from your estate.
* Address any potential estate taxes, if applicable, and outline how these should be covered.

Name an Alternate Executor:

* In case your chosen executor is unable or unwilling to fulfill their duties, designate an alternate executor.

Sign and Date the Will:

* Sign your will in the presence of witnesses. Laws regarding the number of witnesses and their requirements vary by jurisdiction, so check local regulations.
* Generally, two or three adult witnesses are required. Witnesses should not be beneficiaries or related to beneficiaries.
* Each witness should sign and date the will in your presence.

Store and Share the Will:

  * Keep the original will in a safe and secure location, such as a
    fireproof safe or a safety deposit box. Inform your executor
    and a trusted family member or friend where it is stored.
  * Consider providing a copy of the will to your attorney or
    keeping it on file with them.

Review and Update as Needed:

  * Periodically review and update your will to reflect changes in
    your circumstances, such as the birth of a child, marriage,
    divorce, or significant changes in your assets.

Consult with an Attorney:

  * While it's possible to create a simple will on your own,
    consulting with an attorney can ensure that your will complies
    with local laws and regulations and helps avoid potential legal
    challenges.

Balinese Cremation Ceremony

The Balinese Cremation Ceremony, known as "Ngaben," is a unique and intricate ritual that holds great cultural and spiritual significance in Bali, Indonesia. This ceremony is a vivid reflection of the Balinese Hindu belief in the cyclical nature of life, death, and rebirth, and it is an awe-inspiring and communal event that demonstrates the strong sense of community and devotion that characterizes Balinese culture.

The ceremony begins with extensive preparations, often involving the entire village. The deceased's body is first prepared for the cremation. It is placed in an ornate and towering structure called a "wadah" or "bade," which is beautifully decorated with flowers, fabrics, and other offerings. This structure symbolizes the temporary earthly vessel that the soul inhabited.

The procession of the wadah is a grand spectacle. Villagers come together to carry the structure through the streets in a vibrant and colorful parade. The procession is accompanied by traditional Balinese music and dance, creating a lively and festive atmosphere. The purpose of this joyful procession is to confuse malevolent spirits and guide the soul of the departed towards moksha, or spiritual liberation.

The climax of the ceremony is the cremation itself. The wadah is placed on a massive pyre constructed specifically for this purpose. It's often an elaborate structure, intricately designed. The cremation pyre represents the transformation of the soul from the material world to the spiritual realm. Once the pyre is set ablaze, it's believed that the soul is released from the body and begins its journey to the afterlife.

After the cremation, the remaining ashes and bone fragments are collected and placed in a special vessel, usually an intricately carved container. These ashes are often scattered into the sea, a river, or another sacred body of water, symbolizing the return of the soul to its divine source.

The Ngaben ceremony is followed by a series of rituals, including purification rites for the family, prayers, and offerings. It's a time for the community to come together in mourning and to offer support to the family of the deceased.

The Balinese Cremation Ceremony is a remarkable blend of spirituality, artistry, and communal unity. It highlights the Balinese belief in the importance of guiding the soul on its journey to the afterlife and the celebration of a life well-lived. It's a testament to the rich cultural tapestry of Bali and the enduring traditions that make this island so captivating.

Bank

Account

When the Sole Owner of a Bank Account Dies

Notification of Death:

* The first step is to inform the bank about the account holder's death. This can be done by the deceased's next of kin, executor, or someone authorized to act on their behalf.

Account Freeze:

* The bank will often freeze the deceased's account to prevent further transactions until the necessary legal steps are taken. This helps safeguard the assets in the account.

Documentation:

* The bank will request a copy of the death certificate as proof of the account holder's passing. This is a critical document in the process.

Probate or Estate Administration:

* If the deceased had a will, the will's executor or personal representative will typically handle the distribution of assets, including bank accounts, as specified in the will. The will must be filed with the appropriate court for probate or estate administration.
* If there is no will (intestacy), the court will appoint an administrator, and state laws will dictate how the assets are distributed, which often includes bank accounts.

Access to Funds for Immediate Expenses:

* In some cases, the bank may allow the next of kin or the executor to access a portion of the funds for immediate expenses like funeral costs, provided they provide the necessary documentation and legal authorization.

Inventory of Assets:

* The executor or administrator will compile an inventory of the deceased's assets, including bank accounts, as part of the probate or estate administration process.

Transfer of Funds:

* Once the legal process is complete, the funds in the deceased's bank account will be distributed according to the instructions in the will or as determined by state law if there is no will.
* Beneficiaries or heirs named in the will may receive their respective shares, and the remaining funds may be used to settle outstanding debts and expenses of the estate.

Closing the Account:

* After all necessary transactions have occurred, the bank account will be closed. This may involve providing the bank with a copy of the court order granting authority to distribute the assets or other required documentation.

Taxes:

* Depending on the jurisdiction and the size of the estate, there may be estate taxes or inheritance taxes to pay. The executor or administrator is responsible for handling tax matters.

Bank Account Statement:

* The bank will provide a final statement of the account's activity during the probate or estate administration process.

When the Owner of a Joint Bank Account Dies

Joint Tenancy with Right of Survivorship (JTWROS):

* In JTWROS accounts, when one owner dies, the surviving owner(s) automatically becomes the sole owner(s) of the account. This transfer of ownership occurs without the need for probate or court involvement.
* The surviving owner(s) will typically need to provide a copy of the deceased owner's death certificate to the bank to remove the deceased person's name from the account.

Tenants in Common:

* In accounts held as tenants in common, each account holder has a distinct ownership share, which may or may not be equal. When one owner dies, their share of the account becomes part of their estate.
* The deceased owner's share does not automatically transfer to the surviving owner(s). Instead, it will be distributed according to their will or, if there is no will, according to state laws of intestacy.

Community Property:

* In community property states, assets acquired during a marriage are generally considered community property. If one spouse dies, the surviving spouse typically becomes the sole owner of community property assets.
* However, laws regarding community property can vary by state, so it's essential to consult with an attorney for guidance.

Specific Circumstances:

* The specific terms and circumstances of the joint account can affect what happens when one owner dies. For example, some joint accounts may have specific arrangements or restrictions that impact how the account is handled after one owner's death.

Credit Card Debt

Individual Credit Card Debt:

* If the deceased had individual credit card debt with no co-signers or joint account holders, the debt is typically considered a part of their estate.
* The estate is responsible for paying off the deceased's debts, including credit card balances, using the assets left behind.

Joint Credit Card Debt:

* If the deceased had a joint credit card account with another person (e.g., a spouse, family member, or friend), the co-signer or joint account holder may become responsible for the outstanding balance.
* The surviving co-signer or joint account holder should contact the credit card company to discuss the situation. They may be required to continue making payments or negotiate with the issuer.

Authorized User:

* Authorized users on a credit card account are generally not responsible for the debt. The primary account holder is solely responsible.
* If the deceased was the primary account holder, the authorized user is typically not liable for the debt, but they should notify the credit card company about the account holder's passing.

Community Property States:

* In community property states, debts incurred during a marriage are often considered joint debts. This means that a surviving spouse may be responsible for the deceased spouse's credit card debt.
* State laws regarding community property and debt responsibility can vary, so consult with an attorney for guidance if you're in a community property state.

Insolvent Estates:

* If the deceased's estate does not have enough assets to cover their debts, the estate may be considered insolvent.
* In cases of an insolvent estate, creditors may not receive full payment, and the remaining debt may not be passed on to surviving family members or other beneficiaries.

Notification to Creditors:

* Executors or administrators of the deceased's estate are generally responsible for notifying creditors of the person's passing. Creditors have a limited period to make claims against the estate.
* Notify credit card companies promptly to avoid any additional interest or fees on the outstanding debt.

Bank: Account: Contact: Website:
Bank: Account: Contact: Website:
Bank: Account: Contact: Website:
Credit Card: Account: Contact: Website:
Credit Card: Account: Contact: Website:
Credit Card: Account: Contact: Website:

Credit Card:
Account:
Contact:
Website:

Credit Card:
Account:
Contact:
Website:

Credit Card:
Account:
Contact:
Website:

Credit Card:
Account:
Contact:
Website:

Credit Card:
Account:
Contact:
Website:

Credit Card:
Account:
Contact:
Website:

Please tell me you don't have this many credit cards!!!

Zoroastrianism Burial Beliefs

Zoroastrianism, one of the world's oldest religions, has unique burial rituals that reflect its core beliefs in the struggle between good and evil, purity, and the reverence for the elements. The primary Zoroastrian burial practice is known as "sky burial" or "dakhma," which is a fascinating and distinctive ceremony that contrasts with many other burial customs.

Zoroastrian burial takes place in structures called Towers of Silence. These towers are typically located on elevated hills or remote areas to maintain purity and sanctity. The towers consist of raised, open-air platforms or stone circles. The idea behind the Tower of Silence is to expose the deceased to the elements, allowing for the natural process of decomposition while preventing the contamination of the earth, fire, or water, which are considered sacred in Zoroastrianism.

When a Zoroastrian passes away, their body is taken to the Tower of Silence. The corpse is laid out on the platform, exposed to the elements and scavenging birds. Zoroastrians believe that the physical body, once life has left it, is impure and potentially contaminated by evil spirits. Allowing it to decompose through exposure is considered a way to free the soul from its earthly vessel and prevent harm to the sacred elements.

The towers serve as a perch for vultures and other scavenging birds. These birds play a crucial role in the process, as they consume the flesh of the deceased. In Zoroastrianism, these birds are considered "sagdid" or "beneficent birds" because they help in the ritual purification of the body. The remaining bones are bleached by the sun and wind, becoming clean and pure.

The Towers of Silence are considered holy places, and the process of sky burial is regarded with great reverence. Family members and loved ones do not typically attend the burial process itself but may visit the site afterward for prayer and contemplation. It's a time to reflect on the transitory nature of life and the importance of spiritual purity.

Benefits

Benefits for the deceased or those nearing the end of life serve a crucial role in offering support, financial assistance, and peace of mind during challenging times. These benefits are designed to help both the individuals facing the end of life and their families cope with the physical, emotional, and financial burdens that come with such circumstances.

Benefits such as life insurance policies, death benefits, or survivor benefits provide financial relief to the deceased's family, covering funeral expenses, outstanding debts, and ongoing financial responsibilities. They help alleviate the financial strain that may arise from medical bills, end-of-life care, and other expenses incurred during the illness or after the passing.

In situations where the individual's condition may lead to disability or incapacitation before death, benefits such as disability insurance or Social Security Disability Income (SSDI) can offer financial support and assistance with medical expenses, ensuring a better quality of life and easing the financial burdens on the family.

Additionally, various programs and resources, including hospice care, palliative care, and Medicare benefits, aim to enhance the quality of life for individuals facing terminal illnesses. These services focus on providing comfort, pain management, and emotional support for the dying person and their loved ones, enabling them to navigate this challenging phase with dignity and compassion.

Overall, benefits for the dead or dying play a crucial role in providing financial stability, care, and support to individuals facing the end of life and their families, allowing them to focus on spending precious time together and coping with the emotional aspects of this difficult journey.

Social Security

Social Security survivor benefits are a form of financial support provided by the U.S. Social Security Administration to the surviving family members or dependents of a deceased worker who contributed to Social Security during their employment. These benefits offer financial assistance to help families cope with the loss of a breadwinner and the resulting economic hardships.

Survivor benefits primarily cater to the deceased individual's immediate family members, including:

Spouse: A surviving spouse may be eligible for survivor benefits if they were married to the deceased for at least nine months (exceptions apply in certain situations) and are 60 years old or older, or 50 years old if disabled. If the surviving spouse is caring for a child who is under 16 or disabled, they can receive benefits at any age.

Children: Unmarried children under the age of 18 (or up to 19 if still in secondary school) or disabled children may receive survivor benefits. In some cases, stepchildren, grandchildren, or adopted children can also qualify for benefits.

Dependent parents: Parents who were dependent on the deceased for at least half of their financial support may also be eligible for survivor benefits.

The amount of the benefit is calculated based on the deceased individual's earnings and Social Security contributions. Survivors can receive up to 100% of the deceased worker's Social Security benefit, subject to certain limitations.

Applying for Social Security survivor benefits typically involves submitting the necessary documentation to the Social Security Administration, including the deceased worker's death certificate and other relevant information. These benefits aim to provide financial stability and support to families during a difficult period following the loss of a loved one.

Social Security Card

Apply for survivor benefits by calling the Social Security Administration at 800-772-1213 or contact your local Social Security office.

Place your card in a safe along with all your pertinent information.

My card number is:

Veteran's Benefits

Veterans' benefits for widows offer support and assistance to the surviving spouses of deceased veterans. These benefits acknowledge the sacrifices made by the veteran and provide financial assistance and access to various services to the surviving spouse.

Some key benefits available to widows of veterans include:

Dependency and Indemnity Compensation (DIC): DIC is a tax-free monetary benefit paid to eligible survivors of military service members who died in the line of duty or veterans whose death resulted from a service-related injury or illness. It provides monthly financial assistance to the surviving spouse and, in some cases, dependent children.

Pension Benefits: Certain low-income surviving spouses of deceased wartime veterans may qualify for a pension provided by the Department of Veterans Affairs (VA). This benefit is intended to support widows who require financial assistance.

Healthcare Benefits: The VA offers healthcare benefits to eligible surviving spouses through its health care system. This can include hospital care, medical services, mental health services, and more.

Educational Benefits: Some spouses may be eligible for educational assistance programs, such as the Survivors' and Dependents' Educational Assistance (DEA) program, which provides educational and training opportunities.

Home Loan Guaranty: The VA Home Loan Guaranty Program can help surviving spouses secure home loans with favorable terms, including low-interest rates and reduced down payment requirements.

Burial Benefits: Widows of veterans may receive certain burial benefits, such as burial at a national cemetery, a headstone or marker, and burial allowances to cover funeral costs.

Qualification for these benefits often depends on various factors, including the veteran's service record, cause of death, length of marriage, and the surviving spouse's financial situation. Applying for these benefits usually involves submitting documentation, such as marriage certificates, death certificates, military discharge papers, and other supporting documents, to the Department of Veterans Affairs.

VA Information:

Medicare/Medicaid Benefits
Policy Number:

Phone:

Address:

Contact:

Health Insurance
Policy Number:

Group:

Phone:

Address:

Contact:

Secondary Insurance:

Policy Number:

Group:

Phone:

Address:

Retirement Accounts

Retirement accounts are financial vehicles designed to help individuals save for retirement by allowing them to contribute funds that grow over time. When a person passes away, retirement accounts can offer financial support to their surviving spouse or beneficiary, including widows, by providing them with a source of income.

Common types of retirement accounts include:

401(k) Plans: These are employer-sponsored retirement plans that allow employees to contribute a portion of their salary on a tax-deferred basis. If the deceased spouse had a 401(k) and named their spouse as the beneficiary, the surviving spouse may inherit the account and have options such as rolling it into their own retirement account, taking distributions, or leaving it untouched.

Individual Retirement Accounts (IRAs): IRAs are personal retirement accounts that individuals can open independently. Spouses can inherit their deceased partner's IRA, allowing them to continue the account, either as an inherited IRA or by rolling it into their own IRA. Inherited IRAs have specific rules and tax implications that beneficiaries should understand.

Pensions: Some employers offer pensions that provide retirement income to employees. In some cases, pensions can continue to pay benefits to the surviving spouse after the pension holder's death, depending on the pension plan's terms.

For widows, these accounts can offer financial security by providing a source of income. However, the rules and options available to widows regarding inherited retirement accounts can vary based on the specific type of account, the deceased spouse's age at the time of death, and whether required minimum distributions (RMDs) have already begun. It's crucial for widows to understand the rules and implications of inheriting a retirement account to make informed decisions about managing these assets. Consulting with a financial advisor or tax professional can provide valuable guidance in navigating these situations.

Retirement Accounts:

401(k)s, IRAs, pensions, and other retirement savings

Contact Information:

Native American Beliefs

Across the vast expanse of North America, beneath its diverse landscapes and within the hearts of its Indigenous peoples, lies a tapestry of burial beliefs and practices as intricate as the cultures themselves. These traditions are a testament to their profound connection to the land, a reverence for the spirits of ancestors, and an unshakable faith in life's continuity beyond death.

In the heart of this tapestry lies the sacred act of choosing a burial ground. For many Native American tribes, this choice is an affair of the spirit, as the specific location often carries deep spiritual significance. Some tribes prefer the embrace of communal tribal burial grounds, while others seek solace in individual family plots, each a chapter in the history of the land.

Harmonizing with the rhythms of the earth, the circle of life finds expression in the practice of natural burials. Here, the departed find their final resting place directly within the earth's embrace, free from the trappings of embalming or caskets. It is a poignant return to the soil, a poignant reminder of life's cyclical nature.

Facing east, the deceased embarks on a symbolic journey toward the rising sun, a poignant ritual in certain Native American cultures. This directional choice embodies the belief in new beginnings and the passage to the spirit world, a profound moment in the narrative of life and death.

As the body is entrusted to the earth, offerings are made to accompany the soul on its journey. These tokens, be they sustenance, tools, clothing, or objects dear to the individual, serve as guides in the realm beyond, a way of easing the transition from the physical to the spiritual.

In the Southeastern United States, burial mounds stand as mighty testament to the communal nature of Indigenous life. These earthen mounds serve as resting places for multiple souls, carefully crafted over generations, a tribute to the enduring connection between the living and the departed.

In the dance between tradition and change, some Native American tribes embrace cremation. The ashes of the departed find new purpose as they are scattered in places of spiritual significance, *whether a sacred river, an ancient mountaintop, or the very land that cradled their ancestors.*

Rituals unfold in reverent ceremonies, guided by prayers, songs, dances, and the wisdom of tribal elders and spiritual leaders. These rituals light the path to the afterlife, ensuring a safe journey for the departed and honoring their memory among the living.

Respect for the environment is a cornerstone of these practices. Many tribes strive to minimize their ecological impact, opting for eco-friendly burials that echo their reverence for the land. It's a harmonious blend of ancient beliefs and modern sensibilities.

Ancestral continuity is a cherished concept. The spirits of the departed continue to guide, protect, and offer spiritual support to the living, an unbroken bond across the veil of life and death.

Yet, amid this diversity, there's a common thread of respect for the individuality of each tribe's customs. Just as each tribe is unique, so too are their beliefs, their customs, and their ceremonies related to death and burial.

In the modern era, challenges have arisen, especially concerning land use and the protection of sacred burial sites. These challenges serve as poignant reminders of the ongoing importance of preserving and respecting Indigenous burial practices and the rich cultural heritage they embody.

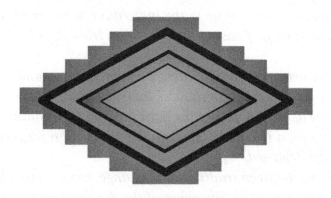

Property
and
Assets

Property and Assets

Cash and Cash Equivalents

Money in checking and savings accounts
Certificates of deposit (CDs)/Money Market Accounts

Real Estate

Primary Residence
Vacation Residence
Rental Properties
Land

Intellectual Property

Copyrights and royalties from creative works (books, music, art)
Trademarks and patents

Property and Assets

Mineral Rights and Royalties

Ownership interests in oil, gas, or mineral rights on land

Royalties from resource extraction

Investments

Stocks and equities

Bonds

Mutual funds

Real estate investment trusts (REITs)

Annuities

Other

Property and Assets

Business Interests

Ownership or equity in a business
Partnership interests

Personal Property

Vehicles (cars, motorcycles, boats, etc.)
Jewelry and valuable collectibles
Furniture and household items
Electronics
Art and Antiques

Cryptocurrencies and Digital Assets

Bitcoin, Ethereum, and other cryptocurrencies
Digital assets such as domain names and online businesses

Mortgage Bank Information
Mortgage Bank Information
Vehicle Loan Information
Vehicle Loan Information
Student Loan Information
Secondary Loan Information
Other Loans
Other Loans

Utilities

and

Bills

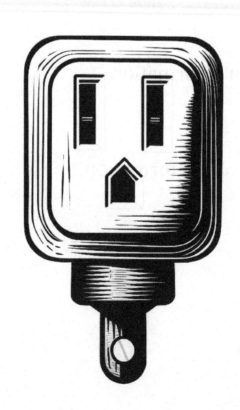

Utilities

Water

Acct #

Phone # 480·

Website

Electricity

Acct #

Phone #

Website

Gas/Propane

Acct #

Phone #

Website

Recycling

Acct #

Phone #

Website

Internet/Cable

Acct #

Phone #

Website

Utilities

Phone

Acct #

Phone #

Website

Auto Insurance

Acct #

Phone #

Website

Home Security

Acct #

Phone #

Website

HOA

Acct #

Phone #

Website

Pest Control

Acct #

Phone #

Website

Utilities

Lawn Care
Acct #
Phone #

Website

Waste Disposal
Acct #
Phone #

Website

Home Warranty
Acct #
Phone #

Website

Health Insurance
Acct #
Phone #

Website

Other
Acct #

Phone #

Website

Utilities

Other

Acct #

Phone #

Website

Other

Acct #

Phone #

Website

Other

Acct #

Phone #

Website

Other

Acct #

Phone #

Website

Other

Acct #

Phone #

Website

Computer and Phone Passwords

Household Notes

The S'Urtzu Tradition: Sardinia's Unique Burial Practices

Nestled in the heart of the Mediterranean, the island of Sardinia is not only known for its stunning landscapes and rich cultural heritage but also for its unique burial practices, most notably the S'Urtzu tradition. These customs, deeply rooted in the island's history, offer a fascinating glimpse into Sardinia's distinct cultural identity.

At the core of Sardinia's burial practices lies the S'Urtzu tradition, which translates to "buried" in the Sardinian language. It's a reflection of the island's strong connection to the land and its long-standing agrarian culture.

Unlike many Western burial practices that involve individual graves, the S'Urtzu tradition often revolves around family mausoleums. These mausoleums are typically constructed from local stone and are intended to house multiple generations of a family.

What sets Sardinia apart is the shared use of these mausoleums. When a family member passes away, they are laid to rest in the same mausoleum as their ancestors. This creates a lasting connection between the living and the deceased, as they share not only a physical space but also a spiritual one.

In some regions of Sardinia, there's a tradition of dressing the deceased in their finest attire. This practice symbolizes respect for the departed and their journey to the afterlife. It's a poignant reminder of the importance of appearances and dignity.

The S'Urtzu tradition is deeply influenced by the island's rural lifestyle. It reflects the values of hard work, family, and the importance of staying connected to one's roots. The mausoleums are not just a final resting place; they are a symbol of continuity.

The S'Urtzu tradition embodies the belief that the deceased continue to watch over and protect their living descendants. It's a comforting thought that reinforces the idea of an enduring family bond, even beyond death.

In recent years, there has been a growing awareness of the need to preserve and protect these unique burial practices. Efforts are underway to safeguard Sardinia's cultural heritage, ensuring that the S'Urtzu tradition continues to thrive.

Sardinia's S'Urtzu tradition is a testament to the island's deep sense of community, family, and reverence for the land. It's a poignant reminder that burial practices are not just about laying the deceased to rest but also about celebrating the enduring connections between generations.

Death
and
Taxes

Death and Taxes

When a spouse passes away, the surviving spouse's tax situation can change based on various factors, including the type and amount of income, assets, and tax filing status. Here's a general overview:

Year of Death: In the year your spouse passes away, you might be eligible to file a joint tax return for that entire year if you remain unmarried for the year. This is known as the year of death filing status. This filing status allows the surviving spouse to use the higher standard deduction and potentially pay lower taxes compared to filing as single or head of household.

Estate Taxes: In the United States, federal estate taxes are levied on the estate of the deceased if it exceeds a certain threshold (which is quite high and changes periodically). Typically, this tax responsibility falls on the estate itself and not the surviving spouse. State laws regarding estate taxes may vary.

Inherited Assets and Income: If you inherit assets or receive income from your deceased spouse, how you're taxed on those assets depends on the type of asset or income:

Inherited Retirement Accounts: Distributions from inherited IRAs or 401(k)s are usually taxable income to the beneficiary. Depending on the type of retirement account and timing of distributions, you might need to pay taxes on these withdrawals.

Inherited Property: Inheriting property generally doesn't trigger immediate taxes. However, if the property is sold in the future, capital gains taxes might apply based on the property's appreciated value.

Life Insurance Proceeds: Life insurance payouts are typically tax-free to the beneficiary, including the surviving spouse.

Filing Status in Subsequent Years: In the tax years following your spouse's death, if you're not remarried by the end of the year, you'll file as a single taxpayer or possibly as a qualifying widow(er) with a dependent child. The tax rates and deductions for these statuses differ from those for married filing jointly.

Given the complexities of tax laws and the different scenarios that may arise, it's advisable to consult with a tax professional or accountant who can provide personalized advice based on your specific situation. They can guide you through the tax implications of inheriting assets, managing income, and filing taxes as a surviving spouse.

Death and Taxes:
Contact my employer for my final W2 form. You will need to file my taxes one last time.
https://www.irs.gov/individuals/deceased-person

Guardianship of a Child

If you wish to establish guardianship for a child before your own death, you can do so through a legal process that ensures the child's care and well-being in the event of your incapacity or passing.
Here are the steps to consider:

Consult an Attorney:

Begin by consulting with an attorney who specializes in family law and guardianship matters. They can provide guidance on the legal requirements and procedures in your jurisdiction.

Select a Guardian:

Choose a suitable guardian for your child. This should be someone you trust to provide the care, love, and support your child needs.

Discuss with the Chosen Guardian:

Have a candid and open discussion with the chosen guardian to ensure they are willing to accept this responsibility. Make sure they understand your wishes and values regarding your child's upbringing.

Prepare Legal Documents:
* Work with your attorney to prepare the necessary legal documents, which typically include:
* Guardianship Appointment: Draft a document that formally designates the chosen guardian for your child.
* Advance Healthcare Directive (Living Will): Specify your wishes regarding medical treatment, particularly if you become incapacitated.
* Power of Attorney: Designate someone to handle your financial and legal affairs if you become unable to do so.
* Will: Ensure that your last will and testament specifies your wishes for the distribution of your assets, including any provisions for the child's care and financial support.

Witnesses and Notarization:

Have the documents witnessed and notarized as required by your jurisdiction's laws.

Share Copies of Documents:

Provide copies of the guardianship appointment and other relevant documents to your chosen guardian, close family members, and your attorney.

Inform Schools and Healthcare Providers:

Notify your child's school, healthcare providers, and any other relevant institutions about the designated guardian and your plans in case of your incapacity or passing.

Review and Update Regularly:

Periodically review and update your legal documents, especially if your circumstances or preferences change.

File Documents with the Court (if required):

Depending on your jurisdiction, you may need to file the guardianship appointment or other relevant documents with the court to make them legally binding.

Consider a Standby Guardian:

In some cases, you may designate a "standby guardian" who can assum responsibility immediately in the event of your incapacity or passing, without the need for court intervention.

Notify Trusted Individuals:

Inform trusted friends or family members about your plans and your chosen guardian. This can be helpful in emergencies.

Legal Consultation for International Guardianship:

If you are an international parent or the chosen guardian resides in a different country, seek legal advice to ensure compliance with international laws.

Remember that guardianship laws and requirements can vary by jurisdiction, so it's crucial to consult with an attorney who is familiar with the laws in your area. Properly executed legal documents provide peace of mind, ensuring that your child's well-being is protected should anything happen to you.

My wishes are...

Guardianship of a Pet

Establishing guardianship for a pet before your death involves making legal arrangements to ensure the care and well-being of your pet when you are no longer able to provide for them. Here are steps to consider:

Choose a Guardian:

Select a responsible and caring individual who is willing and able to take care of your pet. Ensure that they have a genuine affection for your pet and are capable of providing the necessary care.

Discuss with the Chosen Guardian:

Have a conversation with the chosen guardian to confirm their willingness to take on this responsibility. Discuss your pet's needs, routines, medical history, and any special requirements.

Create a Pet Care Plan:

Document your pet's daily routine, dietary preferences, medical history, and any specific care instructions. Include information about your pet's veterinarian, medications, and any allergies.

Draft a Pet Care Agreement:

Work with an attorney experienced in estate planning or pet-related matters to draft a legal agreement specifying the terms of your pet's care.
* This agreement should cover:
* The chosen guardian's responsibilities.
* Instructions for your pet's daily care, feeding, exercise, and medical needs.
* Financial provisions to cover the cost of pet care, including food, grooming, veterinary bills, and other expenses.
* Provisions for the transfer of ownership and any assets or funds designated for your pet's care.
* Contingency plans if the chosen guardian is unable or unwilling to care for your pet.

Include Pet Provisions in Your Will:

Update your will to include provisions for your pet's care and the appointment of the guardian. Ensure that your will specifies how your pet should be cared for and designates funds for their support.

Designate a Pet Trust:

Consider creating a pet trust, a legal entity that holds funds and assets for your pet's benefit. This trust can ensure that resources are available for your pet's care.

Provide Contact Information:

Share contact information for your pet's veterinarian, groomer, and any other essential pet service providers with the chosen guardian.

Emergency Contact List:

Create a list of emergency contacts who can assist in the event of an immediate need for pet care, such as friends or family members who are familiar with your pet.

Update Identification:

Ensure that your pet has proper identification, such as a microchip and tags, and that the contact information is up to date.

Regularly Review and Update:

Periodically review and update your pet care plan and agreements, especially if your pet's needs or your circumstances change.

Communicate Your Wishes:

Share your pet care plan and arrangements with close friends or family members, so they are aware of your wishes.

Consult an Attorney:

Seek legal advice to ensure that your pet care plan and agreements comply with local laws and regulations.

Remember that proper legal documentation is essential to ensure your pet's care when you are no longer able to provide it yourself. Consulting with an attorney who specializes in pet trusts and estate planning can help you create a robust plan for your beloved pet.

My wishes are...

Create a Memory
Preserve a Legacy

Honoring someone's memory and preserving their legacy is a meaningful way to keep their spirit alive and ensure that their impact on the world endures. Here are several ways to achieve this:

Create a Memorial:

Hold a memorial service or gathering to celebrate the person's life and invite family and friends to share their memories and stories.

Establish a Scholarship or Charitable Fund:

Create a scholarship or charitable fund in the person's name to support a cause or organization that was important to them.

Write a Biography or Memoir:

Consider writing a biography or memoir that captures the person's life story, values, and achievements. This can serve as a lasting tribute and historical record.

Build a Memorial Website or Blog:

Create a website or blog dedicated to the person's memory, where you can share photos, stories, and memories. It can be a place for others to contribute their own thoughts.

Plant a Memorial Garden or Tree:

Plant a tree, garden, or flowers in memory of the person. These living memorials can provide a sense of connection and renewal.

Compile a Memory Book:

Collect photographs, letters, and mementos to create a memory book or scrapbook that tells the person's life story.

Hold an Annual Remembrance Event:

Establish an annual event, such as a memorial walk, run, or charity fundraiser, to honor the person's memory and raise awareness for a cause they cared about.

Contribute to Their Passion:

Support or volunteer for a cause, organization, or project that the person was passionate about.

Document Their Wisdom:

Collect and compile the person's writings, advice, or teachings into a book, blog, or social media platform.

Create Art or Music:

Express your feelings and memories through art, music, or poetry dedicated to the person.

Preserve Their Personal Belongings:

Keep and display some of the person's personal belongings, such as clothing, jewelry, or art, as a way to remember them.

Continue Their Legacy of Kindness:

Emulate the person's acts of kindness, generosity, or community involvement in your own life and encourage others to do the same.

Share Their Story:

Share stories and anecdotes about the person with younger generations, ensuring that their legacy lives on through oral tradition.

Support a Cause in Their Name:

Donate time, money, or resources to a cause or charity that was important to the person, dedicating your efforts in their memory.

Create a Documentary or Film:

Produce a documentary or short film that showcases the person's life and contributions.

Leave a Legacy Letter:

Write a letter to future generations or loved ones, sharing your memories and the person's values and lessons.

Encourage Acts of Kindness:

Start a campaign or movement that encourages people to perform acts of kindness in the person's memory.

Educational Initiatives:

Support educational efforts such as workshops, lectures, or classes related to the person's expertise or interests.

Mentorship Programs:

Establish or contribute to mentorship programs in the person's name to help others learn and grow.

Create a Digital Archive:

Build a digital archive of photos, videos, and documents that can be easily accessed and shared with others.

Remember that the most meaningful way to honor someone's memory and preserve their legacy is to continue embodying the values and qualities they held dear. By doing so, you ensure that their impact on the world lives on through your actions and the actions of those you inspire.

Resources

When dealing with the death of a loved one, it's essential to have access to resources that can provide support, guidance, and assistance during this challenging time. Here are some valuable resources for coping with death:

Grief Support Groups:

Local hospices, hospitals, and community centers often host grief support groups where you can connect with others who are experiencing similar losses.

Grief Counseling and Therapy:

Professional therapists and counselors specialize in grief and can provide one-on-one support to help you navigate your emotions and the grieving process.

Books and Literature:

There are numerous books and online resources that offer guidance and insight into grief and mourning. Some well-regarded books include "The Year of Magical Thinking" by Joan Didion and "When Breath Becomes Air" by Paul Kalanithi.

Online Support Communities:

Online forums and communities, such as the Grief Healing Discussion Groups or Reddit's r/GriefSupport, can be sources of comfort and understanding.

Funeral Directors and Services:

Funeral directors can provide guidance on arranging memorial services and handling practical matters related to a loved one's passing.

Legal and Financial Assistance:

Legal professionals can help with wills, estates, and legal matters related to the deceased's assets. Financial advisors can assist with insurance claims and financial planning.

Government and Social Services:

Government agencies and social services organizations can offer support with matters like survivor benefits, social security, and bereavement leave.

Religious and Spiritual Guidance:

If you have religious or spiritual beliefs, your religious community or clergy members can provide emotional and spiritual support.

Memorial and Hospice Services:

Some organizations offer memorial services and hospice care, providing emotional and practical support for individuals facing the end of life.

Advance Planning Services:

Consider services like hospice care or palliative care for those with terminal illnesses. These services focus on enhancing quality of life and providing comfort during the end stages of life.

Estate Planning Attorneys:

Attorneys specializing in estate planning can help navigate legal and financial matters related to a loved one's estate.

Support Hotlines:

Various hotlines, such as the National Suicide Prevention Lifeline (1-800-273-TALK) or the SAMHSA Disaster Distress Helpline (1-800-985-5990), offer assistance during times of crisis or grief.

Remember that seeking help and support is a sign of strength, and it's okay to ask for assistance during this challenging period. You don't have to go through the process of grieving alone, and there are resources available to help you navigate the emotional and practical aspects of dealing with the death of a loved one.

Navigating the wild rollercoaster of losing a loved one is like trying to assemble IKEA furniture blindfolded - you're not entirely sure what's going on, you might hit your thumb with a hammer, and it's going to take way longer than you anticipated. So, cut yourself some slack; this isn't a race, and there are no gold medals for grieving efficiently.

Grief is a bit like the weather in England - unpredictable and occasionally downright miserable. Some days, you'll feel like singing "Don't Worry, Be Happy"; others, you might be auditioning for the role of Eeyore. And that's perfectly okay. Ride those emotional waves however you see fit, whether it involves binge-watching cat videos or crying into a tub of ice cream the size of your sofa.

Don't hesitate to lean on your support squad. Friends, family, or even your neighbor's dog that mysteriously appears in your backyard when you're feeling down can provide comfort. Sometimes, all you need is someone to listen to your ramblings without offering solutions.

With time, the pain might not disappear entirely, but it'll dull a bit, like a pencil that's been through an intense coloring session. Your loved one's memories will become your most cherished treasure, the flickering candle in your darkest moments.

And remember, there's no handbook for this stuff (except this one). So, whether you decide to commemorate your loved one by building a shrine of their favorite snacks or starting an annual "Awkward Family Stories" night, do what feels right for you. Grief is like a fingerprint - unique to each person.

In the end, give yourself permission not to be okay, and understand that you're not alone on this tumultuous journey. You've got a whole world of fellow travelers who've been through their own rollercoasters, and they're here to offer you a hand (or a paw) when you need it most.

Journal

Just a friendly reminder that you're not in this emotional rodeo alone. You've got a fan club of friends and family eagerly waiting for their cue to shower you with love and support. So go ahead, lean on them like a sleepy cat on a sunny windowsill - they're there to catch you when life tosses you a curveball.

Made in the USA
Las Vegas, NV
05 December 2024

13387287R00066